NARBERTH

IMAGES OF THE PAST

Compiled by:

PAULINE GRIFFITHS

and

ANN KEEN

GOMER PRESS IN ASSOCIATION WITH THE WILSON MUSEUM OF NARBERTH

First Impression—1999

ISBN 1 85902 722 9

Printed in Wales at
Gomer Press, Llandysul, Ceredigion

Contents

PREFACE

My grandfather was a Narberth man—Sackville Owen, a land agent with an extensive practice in the county, whose office was opposite the de Rutzen Arms. And so Narberth was my mother's town as well. Now I find myself living only ten miles away and have witnessed in the last dozen years or so Narberth embracing the challenges and opportunities of the day, its gentle—some would say sleepy—past replaced by colourful shop fronts, old buildings revitalised, tourism welcomed, cars (as far as can ever be possible) kept in order and a strong heart beating out from new facilities such as the Queen's Hall and, of course, the Wilson Museum, whose splendid collections have provided the core of material for this wonderful volume.

Yet as these images so forcefully tell us, Narberth has always had a big heart for a small town. The sheer number of people bursting out from the pages, with radiant smiles and carnival costumes, participating in events of national or local interest and captured by the town's industrious local photographers, cause one to linger on each memorable page. And in the street scene photographs, where people are absent, the buildings step forward to take their curtain call too—proudly maintained with their limewash or new cement coats, neat chimney stacks (each one still in use), windows attractive with traditional glazing bars, a riot of different roof pitches, proportions, architectural and decorative styles, the challenge of preserving which (and the character it gives to each individual place) being such an issue everywhere in Britain today.

Several of those who directly shaped the town as architects and builders are rightly mentioned: James Hughes, the town's first architect in the 1820s, who enlarged the church and built in the High Street and John Morgan Thomas, who designed shops and houses in town from the 1870s, both lie in the churchyard. The team who enlarged the town hall in 1912 are rightly remembered along with chapel designers and skilled craftsmen, whose works stand so large in the town's rich built history. No less deserving of their remembering here are the schoolteachers and clergy, who shaped the minds of their generation and the shopkeepers who kept the town up and running. The faces of all those happy classes of schoolchildren and the splendid Noott dance troupers tell us that this was a good time to be young.

There is a famous compliment paid to Narberth from the last century, recalled in H. M. Vaughan's book *The South Wales Squires* (1926), quoting a local gentleman just back from an unsatisfactory holiday in Italy. 'Give me Narberth on a wet Saturday afternoon,' he sighed. And why not? With its historic castle and fine church, its well kept looks, its history lost in the myths of ancient Wales, its good shops and its first class museum, with its wealth of collections that makes it impossible to believe it is a young institution, Narberth has always been a good place to be. My mother's family thought so and I have combed the photographs herein for fleeting glimpses of them. I failed but I know they are in one of those crowd scenes somewhere. Enjoy this book too and lose yourself also among the crowds of your forebears who trod these pavements before you.

Thomas Lloyd
Freestone Hall
Cresselly
(Chairman of the Historic Buildings Council for Wales)

ACKNOWLEDGEMENTS

The Wilson Museum owes a particular debt of gratitude to Mrs Margaret Norris and Miss Ray Davies for their generosity. Ray's efforts over many years, collecting and annotating the postcards, laid the foundations for the publication of this book. Without her it would not have been possible.

Many others have contributed. We have received help and support from the staff in the Record Office in Haverfordwest and from Tenby Museum and Art Gallery whose loan of copies of the *Pembroke County Guardian* has been invaluable. The National Library of Wales kindly allowed us to use copies of photographs from their John Thomas collection.

Several people have contributed their time in order to help us identify faces, locations and events in the postcards. Principal among these have been Mrs Lorna Bees, Mr Harold Cole, Mrs Margaret Eynon, Mr Reg Griffiths, Mr Leslie Owen and Mrs Anne Phillips, although every small piece of information proffered over the years has added to our picture of the town's popular history and we are grateful for that. We hope that this book provokes further reminiscences and that many readers will come forward to record particular memories of Narberth's past.

ABOUT THE POSTCARDS

Sending a postcard in the early part of this century was as much a part of life as phoning or sending e-mail is today. One source estimates that in 1900, 419 million postcards, an average of ten postcards for every man, woman and child in the country, were sent. By 1914 this had doubled.

Narberth, at this time, enjoyed three postal deliveries daily and one on Sunday, so postcards were a quick way to send and receive even everyday news.

With more and more people having the time and opportunity to travel, a demand for postcards as mementoes of holidays and daytrips also increased circulation and, happily for us, postcard-collecting was a popular Edwardian craze.

Several local and national postcard producers stepped in to supply these needs and enough of their work survives to make this book possible.

W. John

William John was born in Penfordd near Clynderwen in 1888. He photographed many of the Narberth street scenes and carnivals that appear in this collection with a 'Special' patent camera made by J. Lancaster of Birmingham that is on display in the museum. His legacy to the area is an invaluable one, especially his recording of the early flight of the James brothers in 1913. Soon after this date, however, he left to work as a shift engineer in the power station of the Great Mountain Colliery in Tumble. He died in 1974 and is buried in Llan-non churchyard.

1. W. John as a young man.

A.F. HALKON

Halkon's newsagents and stationers was in business in Market Square, Narberth from the 1890s on. Many of the earlier postcards, particularly the coloured ones, were published by Arthur Halkon.

H. MORTIMER ALLEN

Third son of renowned Tenby photographer, C.S. Allen, Harry Mortimer Allen was born in 1864. He worked from the 'Excelsior Studio', 1 Campbell House, High Street, Tenby from 1890. In 1896 it was renamed 'The Campbell Studio'. He died in 1926.

ARTHUR SQUIBBS

Born in 1875 in Bridgewater, Arthur Squibbs came to South Wales and had established a studio in Warren Street in Tenby by 1902. From 1906, he worked as the official Tenby and district photographer for the *Daily Express*. He died in 1953.

THE EXCELSIOR STUDIO

Entirely unconnected with Mortimer Allen, this firm was based in Carmarthen.

F. FRITH & COMPANY LTD., REIGATE

The first photographic publishing company in Britain, Frith aimed to cover virtually every town and village in the country. Many local photographers sold their best views to the company which explains the nationwide coverage it achieved. It is not known how many visits were made to Narberth, but several Frith postcards can be dated to 1935.

LILYWHITE LTD.

Working from Sowerby Bridge, Yorkshire, this company also produced photographs of the town in the early 1930s.

JOHN THOMAS

Born in Glan-rhyd, Cellan, Carmarthenshire in 1838, John Thomas left Wales to work in Liverpool when he was 15 years old. Persuaded that there was a need for photographic record of Welsh people and places, he acquired a camera and began what was to become his life's work, '. . . the bringing together of the Great Welshmen and the photographer'. It was important to him to be regarded as an 'artist' for the reputation of a street photographer was not good. 'He would accost you on the street and try to get your order for a few pence and you could hardly get past without having acceded to his request.' His Cambrian Gallery in Liverpool displayed photographs of people and, fortunately for us, places recorded by Thomas that had possibly never been recorded before. Twenty-five such images of Narberth and its surrounding area are kept by the National Library of Wales, three of which we have reproduced with their kind permission.

2. Sheep Fair, Sheep Street, 1890s. This photograph, taken by John Thomas, shows the Old Lion Inn in what is now No. 12, St James Street. The poster in the window reads 'Mr. John Thomas, Artist, Cambrian Gallery, Liverpool, will take photographs here for a short time'.

The postcards here represent only part of the Museum's photographic collection. This book is one way in which that collection can be made more widely available, but visitors and researchers can view the photographs at any time during opening hours.

The information that accompanies the photographs is by no means definitive. We are constantly receiving objects, archive material and anecdotes that add to the always incomplete jigsaw of Narberth's history. We are fortunate that a growing band of 'informants', local Narberth residents and expatriates, continues to provide valuable and previously unrecorded details of life in the town within living memory.

Other sources of information, the newspapers, parish magazines, bill heads, programmes, catalogues and personal reminiscences can also be accessed by students and researchers. By quoting from them here, we hope to give a flavour of some of the material available.

STREETS

M OST of the postcards in our collection show the streets of the town. Evidently the early photographers thought them worth recording even when relatively little seems to be happening

Earlier visitors to the town had not been so impressed '. . . the interior appearance disappoints the expectations excited by the distant view as it is approached', wrote one commentator in 1815. Thirty years later little had changed, 'The houses are irregularly built, and the town presents a very indifferent appearance', was the opinion of whoever wrote Narberth's entry in Robson's trade directory for 1844.

By the early 1870s, however, the town had undergone several improvements. The National (Church) School had been built and the Board (C.P.) School was under construction. Gas lighting had been introduced in 1866 and some older buildings in Market Square were demolished to make way for the Courthouse '. . . a handsome structure, with stone frontage [which] will bear comparison with many public buildings of a like nature in much larger towns'.

The reconstruction continued. St Andrew's Church was rebuilt in 1881, Bethesda Chapel in 1889 and the new Wesleyan Chapel was built in 1905. Indeed, by the end of the 19th century hardly any part of the town remained untouched. 'Our little town is looking up', wrote the Rev. John Morris in the Parish Magazine of 1897. 'The improvement in the houses in Sheep Street, St James Street, Market Street and High Street is a striking one, and has given employment to a number of masons, plasterers and carpenters during the summer'. A year later he added, 'Anyone who has not recently passed along the Plaindealings (Northfield) Road would hardly know that once miserable, poverty-stricken, dirty neighbourhood. The new owners of the old hovels have pulled them down and are erecting good, substantial dwellings all along the road'.

While the fabric of the buildings was upgraded, the state of the streets themselves left a lot to be desired. 'Church Street is a disgrace to any civilised town. Pools of muddy water, filthy refuse of all kinds covers the roadway, whilst the so-called pavement is used as a convenient resting place for the carts of the parish thus compelling foot passengers to use the filthy street . . . The Station Road, too, is a sea of mud . . . What an idea strangers must form of us. No wonder they call our little town, as the writer has heard it called, "Dirty Little Narberth".'

Of course, the town grew in prosperity as a result of its location and its markets and fairs which feature significantly in our postcard collection. 'The town on market day', wrote one observer in 1868, 'assumes a complete air of bustle and activity, thronged as it is on that day by the presence of hundreds of the country people who, attired in all the varieties of Welsh costume, conduct their bargains and sales chiefly in the native language'. The history of the market has been covered in *The Story of Narberth*. Baron de Rutzen's market hall, built in 1833, never entirely overcame the townspeople's understandable desire to buy and sell goods more cheaply in the square and surrounding streets. A newspaper report of 1898 spelt out the problems this could cause. 'An intolerable nuisance is committed market day after market day during the fish season by mackerel vendors being allowed to stand the whole day on the square with their boxes of fish, from which water is oozing and causing a fearful stench, which lasts for a couple of days afterwards . . . Those in authority seem powerless in the matter and shift their responsibility. The Sanitary Inspector says he has nothing to do with it, and must go to the Road Surveyor. The latter in his turn says you must go to the Police, and on consulting the Police, they say they have nothing to do with "stinks".'

The market hall was enlarged in 1897 and renamed the Victoria Hall. An ambitious building, it doubled as a covered market and public hall and was described as the biggest of its kind this side of Llanelli. A concert was given there during the Jubilee celebrations and '. . . the size of this new hall may be better understood when we say that the audience of about 1,200 did not nearly fill the room'.

Fairs were held with increasing frequency throughout the period. By the turn of the century they were held monthly with the addition of the hiring fair in October. They brought colour, excitement, trade and employment to the town. Food, drink and accommodation were provided in the numerous pubs and hotels many of which still exist with their original names. The fairs brought a degree of disruption too, of course, and the railings outside many of the properties to which the animals were tethered were intended to keep them out of the houses.

The schools were particularly badly affected on fair days. Many pupils played truant because of the casual work available around the town. Others stayed away, drawn by what the headteacher of the Board school described as '. . . So many attractions outside in the shape of shows, swingboats, Galloping Horses etc.' Frequent entries in the logbook echo this complaint. 'These fairs are the bane of the school. There are so many cattle and horse about the streets that parents will not send their children to school'. It was hoped that the Mart or Fair ground opened in Spring Gardens around 1910 would ease the problem but, as this 1911 entry records '. . . the horses and colts have not been removed from the school's precincts and these – the parents say – constitute the danger to life'.

As cars and other motor vehicles replace the horses in the later photographs, the 'danger to life' alters. The streets themselves remain much the same. The fascination of these postcards lies in the evidence they provide of the changing histories enacted against that backdrop.

3. High Street, late 19th century, the earliest view we have of the lower end of High Street. J.D. Lewis' ironmongers (right), was the forerunner of Lewis and John which moved to Spring Gardens around 1907. R.H. Davies' draper's shop, The Golden Sheaf, can be seen (left). The buildings behind the townhall, the Globe Temperance Hotel and Albert House, have since been demolished.

High Street — Narberth

4. High Street, showing the town hall before it was extended in 1912. The main building dates from 1833 when records describe 'A lock-up house, having over it a room in which magisterial and parochial meetings are held'. The clock was made by J.W. Benson in 1880. Note the Post Office (left) before it was relocated in Spring Gardens in the early 1920s. It had also, around 1884, been situated in St. James Street.

5. High Street. Card is postmarked 1922. The business on the left had been the premises of Philip Wheeler, undertaker and cabinetmaker, whose life and times are described in his grand-daughter's memoir *My Father was a Narberth Man*. At the time of this photograph the shop was kept by T. Griffiths and Sons, wholesale ironmonger.

6. High Street, mid-twentieth century. In 1976, Mr T.J. Adams wrote to *The Western Telegraph*:
'In the Spring and Summer of 1912, I was one of the builders, the other being Mr. Thomas Hughes of Robeston Wathen, who built the second storey of (what was then known as) the Mechanics Institute'. He names the other craftsmen involved and continues 'The building stones at both ends came from Robeston Wathen quarry. The side walls were of brickwork . . . the roof of the old building was removed and fixed on the new building, including all the Caernarvon slates, which are still on the roof. The contractor was Mr. Williams, Brynhelen, Robeston Wathen, who also did the carpentry work. Mr. George Thomas, Templeton . . . drew the plans and specifications and also gave a tender for the work. The contract price was less than £140.'

7. The Golden Sheaf, beginning of the century. Principally a draper's and haberdasher's shop, this photograph shows a variety of other goods on sale, eg. rolls of lino. A cloak made here at about this time can be seen at the museum. The Conduit Inn (right), named because of its proximity to one of the water sources in the town, was kept by J. Davies at this time.

8. Crowd in High Street, early years of the century. Frustratingly, we do not know the reason for this gathering but it may well have been a political meeting. A particularly turbulent scene was witnessed in July 1908 when several candidates for election, including Mrs Pankhurst, visited the town. Their arguments seem to have gone unheard, as 'Deafening roars and catcalls emanated from hundreds of rival party adherents, and women savagely contributed hideous discords by beating old tin pans and jugs'. The event did not go unrecorded apparently for '... photographers courageously secured points of vantage on house tops and public lamp posts, and the following day the London and provincial dailies produced splendid pictures of the scene'. Could this be one?

9. View down High Street, early years of the century. The Angel Hotel is mentioned in Pigot's *Directory* of 1830. Its stables were demolished when the Queen's Hall was built.

10. Early view of Narberth Fair on a card postmarked 1904. Note the railings erected to prevent intrusion by the animals tethered for sale. Havard's Pharmaceutical Chemist, (left with windows draped), was first listed in 1868. The King's Arms, (extreme left), later became a temperance hotel.

11. High Street, just after the First World War. The Angel Hotel (centre background) can be seen before it was extended into the cottage next door. Next door down is the shop of A.G. Owen, tailor, and next to that is the Star Supply Stores. One of a chain of grocery shops, it was established in Narberth by 1914.

12. Top of High Street. Royce Lewis, seen standing by the telegraph pole, remembers the photograph being taken in 1935. The sheep, making their way to the Mart ground or to the station, belonged to Mr Eynon, the last licensee of the Old Eagle in Church Street. The Ivy Bush (behind van) has been there from 1868 at least. William Roblin kept the newsagent in Milton House, next door, and the jeweller's shop by the signpost was owned by D.J. Edwards.

13. Top of High Street, looking up Spring Gardens, between 1907-1910. Although the children are probably from the Board school, we do not know why they are gathered here on this occasion. The Coach and Horses (right) is recorded in Slater's *Directory* of 1868. At the time of the photograph it was kept by Arthur Evan Thomas. Hill House is just visible behind the trees (left).

14. Looking up Moorfield Road, early years of the century. The school, designed by J.M. Thomas, a Narberth architect, was built in 1872. Only this terse comment in the school's log book for May 15th, 1874 commemorates its opening:

'Commenced School in the New Room. Obliged to depart from Time Table in order to re-arrange school.'

The School was extended in 1906 and the new work can be seen here.This too caused the same disruption

'Removed children this morning to the old British schoolroom [Tabernacle vestry] to be held there until the new building has been completed.'

The houses in Moorfield [Park] Terrace (right) date from at least 1835. Behind the trees in the background is the rectory, Belmore House, now the Plas Hyfryd Hotel.

15. Hill House and Moorfield Terrace, early part of the century. The house dates from the late eighteenth century, making it one of the oldest in town. It has been an estate agent's office for many years.

16. Top of High Street, late 1930s / early 1940s. Note the chimneys which have now been removed from the school and the railings to which horses were tied on Fair days. The frontage of Hill House has also been opened up.

Plain Dealings Road Narberth

17. Plaindealings (Northfield) Road, early years of the century. The corn store (left) continued to be used into the 1920s by Norman Collins. Percy Harkett's wheelwright business was in this road as was John James' smithy, later taken over by his son, Tommy.

Spring Gardens, Narberth.

Copyright.
Nbh. 14.

18. Spring Gardens, early 1930s. The cottages next door to the Post Office were demolished to make way for an extension which was officially opened on 20th March, 1936. Sidney Jenkins had kept a shop in one of them. Note that, on the left of the photograph, milk is still being deliversd in churns although milk bottles were introduced into Britain around 1906.

19. View of Spring Gardens, 1950s. The extension to the Post Office is clearly visible. The Farmer's Arms, a relatively 'new' Narberth pub, is shown in 1871 as being run by a John Williams.

20. William Williams outside his flannel shop, Bradford House, in Spring Gardens, c.1920. Welsh flannel, woven locally, was one of the many items sold here. The business was continued for a time by his son, Idris.

21. Spring Gardens, early 1920s, showing James John, ironmongers (left). The firm, previously known as Lewis and John, had moved from the High Street by 1907 when the building of the new Mart ground in Cross Lanes [Spring Gardens] was being proposed. Thomas Picton kept a grocer's shop (right) from around 1914 until 1923.

22. Houses in Jesse Road, early 1930s. The road takes its name from Jesse's Well and the cottages opposite. The houses here are shown shortly after they were built by Thomas Morgan of Northfield Road.

23. View of Wesley Villas, Station Road, 1920s. The Methodist Chapel, after which they were named can be seen in the background. Built in 1905 by Thomas Griffiths, Master builder, at a cost of £850, it no longer has the spire visible in this photograph and is now the Masonic meeting place.

24. Station Road, early 1930s. The Commercial Inn (left background) had previously been The Gate, built in 1833 and named after the tollgate sited here in the early part of the 19th century.

25. Commercial Corner, late 1930s. The shop on the left was kept by Alfred Voyle before being taken over by Mr. R. Reynolds. Eastgate House (right) had been a school in the middle of the nineteenth century. At the time of the photograph it was a clinic where Nurse Parish was district nurse for many years.

26. Sheep Street, early years of the century. George Fisher kept a grocer's in the shop shown on the left. The last building on the left-hand side of the street was the Butcher's Arms, a public house and brewery kept by David Phillips in 1914.

27. Tom Evan's grocery shop in St James Street, about 1920. The owner (centre) is shown with his nephew, Ronnie John (left) and son, Jackie (right). Jackie's own son, Eric Evans, became Dean of St Paul's in London. They are pictured outside Dudwell House, although the shop was often known as the Brook shop, taking its name from Brook House, the family home next door. The identities of the children are not known.

28. St. James Street below Tabernacle Lane. Card is postmarked 1914. C.G. Thompson kept a draper's in London House (left) and his engraved glass sign can still be seen. Staunton House Refreshment Rooms are on the right.

29. Sheep Street, 1910. The building of the Mart ground gradually removed the sale of animals from Narberth streets but this did not happen immediately. The bay-windowed shop on the left belonged to W. Edwards, tailor.

ST JAMES' ST. NARBERTH.

30. Market Square, early part of the century. Crockery and china were sold at this spot for many years by Mr. T. Sheen. The town crier, George Phillips of Church Street, can be seen in the background, his head level with the awning.

31. Market Square, early twentieth century. It is not known exactly why so many people are gathered here on this occasion, but the *Weekly News* carried this advertisement on 5th May 1910:

'Market Square, Narberth – Highly important sale of New and Second Hand Carriages, Traps, Farm carts, Farm implements, Wheelbarrows and other effects. Mr. W. Palmer Morgan has been instructed to sell by Public Auction at the above place on Fair Day 11th May, 1910'.

Other evidence suggests this may be a postcard of that sale.

32. Market Square. The card is postmarked 1906. W. Palmer Morgan kept the chemist's in Market Square from around the turn of the century.

The lamp clearly visible in all postcards of Market Square has been the subject of much speculation. A report in the *Pembroke County Guardian* on May 26th, 1900 casts some light on the subject.

'On the news of the relief of Mafeking reaching Narberth, everyone seemed overflowing with patriotism, and every house displayed bunting. A newly erected electric lamp, which is situated outside the premises of Mr. J. L. H. Williams, was shown to great advantage, and especially so since it was the first time for it to be lit.'

33. Market Square. Card postmarked 1907. Number 14 Market Square on the immediate left of this picture was, at this time, the home of James Williams and his family. It was his pioneering work that brought electricity to Narberth. The building had previously housed the White Lion, one of the oldest inns in the town. Next door is Brownlee Boot and Shoe Warehouse, a business that was there from around 1889. J.W. Davies kept the grocery shop and next door to that was the Globe Temperance Hotel owned by T. Sheldon. Re-named Noklah House when it was owned by the Halkon family, it was demolished in the 1970s.

34. Market Square, turn of the century. The businesses from the left are Henry Adams, fried fish dealer; E. Morris, clothiers; W. Palmer Morgan, chemist; A. F. Halkon, newsagent and stationer and B. Eynon, a long-established jeweller and watch repairer.

It was A.F. Halkon, publisher of many of the early postcards in this book, who endeared himself to readers nationwide in 1987 when it emerged that his son, Ron Halkon, intended to donate his father's 'Penny- Farthing' style bike to the museum. The bike, properly known as a 'Geared Facile', was ridden by Arthur Halkon from Birmingham to Narberth in 1886, 120 miles, to see his bride-to-be, Margaret Sheldon. Following a lengthy restoration, the bike, one of only 'six in the world', is now on display in the museum.

35. View from Market Square looking down Market Street, early 1900s. William Burgess, an Oxford-born man who served his apprenticeship at the Oxford University Press, set up his printing business in Narberth around 1902. The first edition of the *Narberth, Whitland and Clynderwen Weekly News* was published on Thursday, March 15th, 1906.

The Courthouse, on the right of the picture, was designed by Charles Reeves of London, H.M. Surveyor of Police and County Courts. The builders were Morgan, Howell and Williams of Carmarthen and it was built in 1864 at a cost of £3,000.

36. Narberth War Memorial, Friday, 14th March, 1924. The site for the memorial was donated by Capt. J.H.L. Williams and the architects were Major Hugh Thomas of Haverfordwest and his assistant Capt. Ingleton. Funds were raised by a committee of local people.

37. Narberth War Memorial, Market Square. The unveiling was performed by Private Albert Nicholas, a Narberth man, of the 15th Welsh Regiment who had lost a lung and both his legs while serving in France.

One of the masons who worked on the memorial, Mr. Arnold Jenkins of Redford House, recalled '... great blocks of granite coming down from Aberdeen where they had been made into sections. We had to lift them off the trucks by crane and down onto a massive four-wheeled wagon drawn by two great cart horses. We then unloaded them on site by sliding them off sideways down thick planks of wood using crowbars as levers ... and I can tell you that was back-breaking work.'

But the biggest problem was setting the cross on the top. 'No one wanted the job because it was so heavy and a bit risky to climb the ladder and ease the dowel at its base down into the neck of the shaft. So we all sat round and scratched our heads. In the end, Tom Griffiths – who must have been all of seventy years old and a stone mason himself – got up the ladder and we hauled the cross up to him with ropes and pulleys'.

38. St Andrew's Church, Narberth. Card postmarked 1922. The oldest part of the church dates from the late twelfth/early thirteenth century but there have been major alterations since that time – in 1828 by James Hughes, the Narberth architect and builder and again in 1881 by T. G. Jackson. The gates were cast in 1856 by Messrs. Morgan and Thomas of Narberth but the railings, paid for by public subscription, came later. Writing in 1897, the Rev. John Morris described how a '... dwarf limestone wall surmounted by five feet iron railings on either side of the entrance gates replaces the hideous old wall of eight feet high which hid and completely dwarfed this handsome church'.

39. Bethesda Baptist Church, High Street. The original chapel was built in 1837, although the Baptist cause in Narberth dates back to 1808. The present chapel, opened in 1891, was designed by Mr. John Williams, Architect, of Ingledew House, Narberth and built by Messrs. Williams and sons of Robeston Wathen. *The Pembroke County Guardian* report quotes a cost of £1,888.17s 4d which was met largely by donations from Narberth residents and '. . . From persons who belonged to Narberth but who were now settled in distant towns in various parts of the world'.

40. Crinow Church, Crinow. In 1901, the churchyard was extended in a ceremony which incorporated a memorial service for Mr Charles Sheild, who died on board his ship while passing through the Red Sea. In the centre of the new portion of the churchyard donated by Mr and Mrs Sheild of Parcglas, a marble monument was erected in memory of their son.

41. Wesleyan Church, Station Road. Built in 1905 by Thomas Griffiths, Master Builder, at a cost of £850, the architect was J. Preece Jones. The steeple has since been removed.

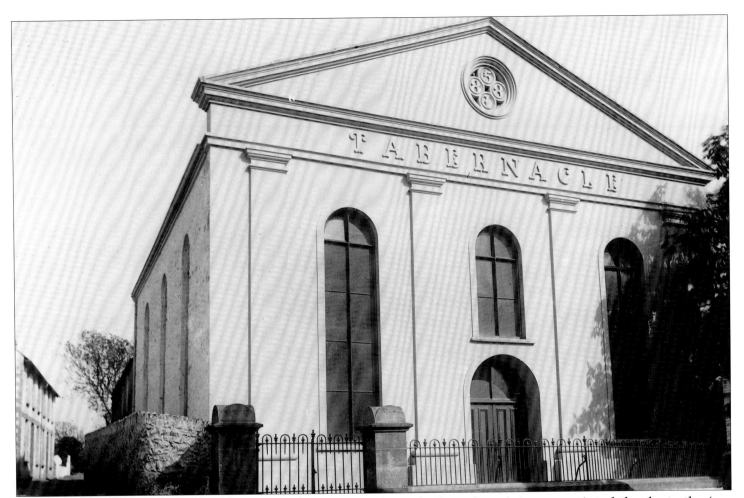

42. Tabernacle Chapel, Occupation Lane. In 1819 a chapel was built and a minister appointed thanks to the '... earnest and generous spirit of one individual' who bore the whole cost himself but chose to remain anonymous. The congregation outgrew this original building which then became the vestry and the location of the British School. The foundation stone of the present chapel was laid in 1858. The cost, including the site (on which the Rev. Henry Davies' house had stood) was estimated to be '... not less than £1,000'.

CARNIVALS

Very little is known about the early carnivals. There appears to have been scant newspaper coverage during the first decade of the century and, were it not for the postcards, many taken by W. John of Clynderwen, we would have no record of what was obviously a popular and well-attended civic event. This tantalisingly brief account from the *Pembroke County Guardian* of 1906 tells us little about the organisation of the carnival, except that it was held in September.

CARNIVAL AT NARBERTH.

A very successful carnival was held at Narberth last Saturday, the results being as follows :—

EQUESTRIAN IN COSTUME—Winners, T. Griffiths and E. Price ; special, E. Owen.

PEDESTRIAN IN MALE COSTUME—1st, W. Mathias ; 2nd, H. Phillips.

PEDESTRIAN IN FEMALE COSTUME—1st, Miss Mary Davies ; 2nd, Miss Webb.

PEDESTRIAN IN COSTUME (ladies only)—Miss Emily Owen.

BEST DISGUISE—1st, Trevor Reynolds ; 2nd, David Williams.

DECORATED CAR—1st, —. Rees, Narberth ; 2nd, S. Rowlands ; 3rd, F. Bowen.

DECORATED CYCLE—1st, Miss Mary Davies ; 2nd, Charles Davies.

COSTUME (girls under fifteen)—1st, Mary Davies ; 2nd, Nellie Davies.

FANCY COSTUME (children)—1st, Sibby Phillips ; 2nd, Ena Rees ; special, brothers O'Neill.

WELSH COSTUME—1st, Miss Polly Winstone ; 2nd, Miss Maud Britton.

PEDESTRIAN IN CHARACTER COSTUME—1st, —. Thorpe ; 2nd, S. Rowlands.

ILLUMINATED CAR—1st, " Black Dike Band " ; 2nd, —. Rees, Narberth.

ILLUMINATED CYCLE—1st, Ll, Griffiths ; 2nd, Miss Mary Davies.

ILLUMINATED HOUSE—Miss Martha Evans.

Nearest guess to total amount collected in boxes during the day—Miss Mary Ann Lloyd, whose figure was 1½d. short of the actual amount collected

What we can tell from the photographs is that in these early years, the procession appears to have ended at the castle where the judging also seems to have taken place. The variety of the costumes and resourcefulness of the entrants is remarkable given that there was so much less inspiration from outside influences than today.

Pictorial evidence exists to show that carnivals were held into the 1920s. *The Pembrokeshire County and West Wales Guardian* of July, 1928 reported:

'A grand carnival, in aid of the Womens' Institute Hut Fund, was held in Narberth on Saturday, the 14th inst., under extremely favourable weather conditions. The competitors assembled in the Cricket Field at 2.30. pm, where a procession was formed. It wended its way through the principal streets, and returned to the Cricket Field where the judging took place ... In point of numbers and variety, the carnival was a success, and a large number of people assembled in the strees to inspect the quaint get-ups, grotesque characters, beautiful costumes etc. There were very few competitors in the decorated and descriptive vehicle classes. There was only one decorated motor car, and only one descriptive turn-out. The entries in the classes for pedestrians in character and fancy costumes were numerous, and most of the dresses were artistic and original.

The scene on the cricket Field when all the competitors marched past the judges was a truly picturesque one.'

In *The West Wales Guardian* of July 1938, a reference to the 'annual carnival' suggests they were held earlier in the decade although we have found no reports describing them. That year's queen was Mercia Charlton and the winning float, 'A lorry decorated to form a small hut with Snow White and the Seven Dwarfs . . . arranged by Mr Charles Salmon'. In 1944, the Carnival, as usual arranged by the W.I., was held in the cricket field. Betty Christopher, the Queen, was attended by Mary Allen, Mary Bevan, Olive Carr, Gwendoline de Winton, Margaret Rees and Merle Scourfield. The proceedings included an opening ceremony, a procession round the town and amusements in the Fun Fair.

The 1945 Victory carnival was notably filmed by Stanley Lewis. A remarkable record of the times, it shows American servicemen who were stationed in the down during the War. The film, transferred onto video, has been shown in the Museum during recent civic week celebrations.

The popularity and fame of the carnival has continued to grow. In 1999 the television presenter, Roy Noble, spent a week in the town filming the events of Civic Week and interviewing participants in the carnival itself for his popular television series, aptly named *On Common Ground*.

There is no reason to doubt that, having endured for the last one hundred years, the opportunity for communal anarchy that is Narberth Carnival will continue well into the next Millennium.

43. Carnival procession, High Street, 1906. Note the Carnival Queen in the horse-drawn decorated cart.

NARBERTH CARNIVAL. 1906 W, J.

44. The procession at the bottom of Market Street, 1906. The Castle Hotel, on the left, was kept by F. Child. Other businesses in Market Street at this time were W.E. Jenkins, grocer; S. Jones, saddler; H.V. Thomas, cabinet-maker and G. Williams, decorator.

45. Castle grounds, 1909. A selection of carnival entrants. The lady on the left, Miss Emily Owen, appears to have entered the 'decorated cycle' competition several years in succession. The gentleman on horseback dressed as Charles the Second is F.H. Lewis, father of Stanley Lewis, the pioneering electronics engineer.

46. Carnival group, 1907. Mounted entrants await judgement.

NARBERTH CARNIVAL, 1907 W G MORRIS

47. Castle Field, 1906. Groups line up for the judges' decision. The houses of Church Street and Castle Street can be seen in the background.

48. Carnival procession at the top of High Street, 1908.

49. Judging at the Castle Field, 1907. The signs on the decorated cart read: 'Blood and Thunder', 'Home-brewed beer and sausages round the corner' and 'Jug and Bottle Dept.'

50. Unknown Carnival entrant, perhaps the forerunner of our 'Rose Queen' ?

51. Castle grounds, 1908. This banner appears in Carnival processions on several occasions.

52. Carnival procession, High Street, 1909. The small decorated cart reads 'Nicholas and Farror, Motor Engineers'.

53. Entrants in the 'Decorated bicycle' class, 1909.

54. Carnival procession, bottom of Market Street, 1910. The large barrage balloon-like structure reads 'Oakhill Stout'.

55. Decorated cart. Castle Field, 1910. Jack or Johnny Williams is 'Dr. Gorgonzola trying his own medicine'. The gentleman holding the horse is William Irving.

56. Entrants in the Children's Fancy Dress competition, 1907. Howard James, one of the pioneering aviators from Clynderwen, can be seen at the back on the extreme right.

57. High Street, 1919. The cart (left foreground) reads 'Don't forget the old firm' and appears to be selling biscuits. As might be expected, there are several entrants in military uniform.

58. High Street, 1920s. The bus carries the advertisement 'Ross. Every Man To His Job. The Live Wire of Local Wireless' and covers the Tenby-Narberth-Haverfordwest route. Note the Pratt's petrol pump on the left of the street. Their depot was at Kiln Park cottage. The Angel Hotel (centre background) has been extended into the cottage next-door.

SCHOOLS

SCHOOL photographs form a large proportion of the Wilson Museum collection. The survival of such photographs is not difficult to explain – many copies would have been produced and, in a time before mass popular photography, cherished as perhaps the only record of childhood.

Three Narberth schools are represented here: the Board School, the National School and the Intermediate School. What is their history?

Before the 1850s, the only free or affordable education available was in Charity and Sunday Schools. The Devonald Trust, created in 1832, provided £30 for the education of poor children and with this money a cottage was at first rented for use as a schoolroom. In 1837 the old poorhouse at Narberth Bridge became vacant when the new Union Workhouse was built at Allensbank. The Devonald Charity school was moved there after the Rector had spent £40 repairing and renovating the building. The inspectors who visited the school in 1846 were, on the whole, favourably impressed with the way the school was run although they deplored the lack of books. Attempts to encourage voluntary contributions from parents to improve the facilities had failed because 'The common people of the place are wretchedly poor, and cannot spare money or even their children for school . . .'

Several private schools existed at this time. A grammar school at Eastgate House charged £25 a year for boarders and 10/6d a quarter for day-scholars. The inspectors noted that 'Many enter the school who know no English.'

Other schools were held in private houses around the town and also at the Union Workhouse where 'All the clothes used in the house are made'. At Mrs Arundel's school in Island House (Market Square, now demolished), 'The samplers appeared to be worked very neatly and with great care'. Conditions in Mr Joseph's day-school in Sheep Street were less impressive. The smell in the small room was '. . . quite overpowering'. The master, unable to walk since childhood, kept control of the class from the middle of the room with the aid of a 6-foot rod. There were two other schools mentioned by the Inspectors: Mrs Owen's in Sheep Street and Miss Thomas' in Picton Terrace.

By the middle of the 19th century a more standardised approach to education was beginning to emerge nationally. The National Society (For The Education Of The Poor In The Principles Of The Established Church) had set up schools throughout the UK and by 1850 a 'National School' existed in Narberth. Its whereabouts are unknown but its shortcomings were described in an Inspectors' report of 1863. 'The present school affords but limited accommodation and is also rather inconveniently situated at some distance from the town. The desks and other fixtures are old and in imperfect repair. A new schoolroom on a more airy and central site would be of great benefit.'

Such a school was built and established by 1850 and still stands in Church Street. It later became popularly known as the Church School, but was closed around 1968. Since 1981, the building has housed the Roman Catholic Church of the Immaculate Conception.

The British and Foreign Schools Society had maintained a school in the old Tabernacle Chapel from around 1865. Known as the British School, it provided non-doctrinal, non-denominational education.

The 1870 Education Act provided for the election of school boards made up of local people who would levy rates to build and maintain schools. In 1873, a 'Board School' was built near the Town Moor. It was extended in 1905 and renamed the Council School.

Rivalry between the two primary schools was intense and involved staff as well as pupils. A constant complaint was that children, aggrieved by their treatment in one school, would simply turn up at the other.

In 1905, around the time many of these photographs were taken, the headmaster of the Board school, Mr J. Harries, wrote in his log:

'Katie John, who was caned on the hand for neglect and inattention went to the National School in the afternoon. A note was sent to the Headmaster there reminding him of the covenant made long ago between us as to dealing with such cases and pointing out to him how, in similar instances, a boy was not admitted here and also that this child left here without the knowledge of the father'.

The Intermediate School also came into existence as a result of an Act of Parliament. The first headmaster, John Morgan, had, since 1888, held a private grammar school in a house next to his lodgings and then in the old British School. In 1889, the Welsh Intermediate Education Act made recommendations for the provision of secondary education giving instruction in English, Mathematics, Modern languages, Classics, Elementary Science and Scripture. The Narberth County Intermediate School was opened in June 1896. It was initially intended for 80 pupils (50 boys and 30 girls). A large proportion of the pupils who travelled from rural areas stayed in lodgings in the town during the week. Many of them were Welsh-speaking and felt that their hosts and the town children looked coldly on them. Even some of the teachers made them feel uncomfortable about their Welshness.

Pupils had to pay tuition fees but Narberth's were the lowest in Pembrokeshire at £3 6s (including stationery, but £1 11s 6d extra for music). Teachers at the County Intermediate School were also comparatively better paid and there was less turnover of staff.

At first the majority of the pupils were the children of farmers and tradesmen but with the increase in the number of scholarships more children of working class parents were enabled to attend although many were removed before their education was completed.

The school produced some notable pupils. Thomas Benjamin Wheeler, who obtained his Honours certificate at the school in 1904/5, became a Fellow of the University of Wales and later Chief Education Officer of Middlesex. Roger Thomas gained a first class honours degree in Botany at Aberystwyth and went on to become an esteemed agricultural adviser in India. He was made a member of the cabinet of government in Sind in 1944 and was knighted in 1947. William Thomas, having obtained his Senior Certificate in 1908 followed a glittering academic career before becoming Chief Inspector of Schools in Wales. Waldo Williams, the eminent and much-loved poet, whose most famous collection, *Dail Pren* ('Leaves of a Tree'), included poems written in response to the Second World War and the Korean War, was at the school during John Morgan's last year.

John Morgan seems to have inspired affection and loyalty in everyone who came into contact with him. He himself admitted that he was not very good at class control by the standards of the time. But as his biographer, Abel Jones wrote:

'I often expressed the view that a good disciplinarian must have a little of the devil in him, at least enough to perceive the demon in others and enough to insist that others obey him when he commands. John Morgan had not enough of this to be a strong disciplinarian.'

If this was a fault then it appears to have been his only one. Abel Jones' biography, available in the Museum library, gives numerous examples of John Morgan's kindness, his generosity and his devotion to his pupils. A portrait of him, painted by a former pupil, Mary Sinclair Morgan, hangs in the Museum.

The Intermediate School, later Narberth Grammar School and finally Narberth County Secondary School, closed in 1986.

59. Narberth Council School, sometime after 1906, when the name of the school had been changed from the Board School. Staff: Miss Howells (right) and Miss Gwendoline Cole (left).

60. Narberth Council School. As before.

61. Narberth Council School, 1927. The infants' class with headmistress, Miss Kate Edwards (centre), Miss Cole (left) and Miss John (right).

62. Narberth Church School, early 1920s. Younger pupils with Miss Alie Owen (right) and Miss Lilian Bowen (left).

63. Narberth Church School, c. 1918. Headmaster Mr Frederick Bowen. Stanley Lewis (back row, extreme right) went on to become a pioneering electrical engineer.

64. Narberth Church School, 1926. Headmaster Mr Frederick Bowen and Miss Purser.
Back row (from left): Hughie Owen, Eric Davies, Eddie Mathias, Clive Cook, Joan Baker, Marjorie Baker.
Middle row (from left): Clifford James, Betty Holmes, Lorna Irving, Glenys Watkins, ? , Claude Phillips.
Seated (from left): Ruth James, Joan Watkins, ? , ? , Glenys Irving, Joyce Davies, Glenys Jenkins, Beryl Lewis, Joyce Prior, Dorothy Narbett, Lizzie Lewis, Phyllis Roberts, Winnie Roberts.
Front row (from left): ? , Howard Christopher, Oliver Evans, ? , Eric Gaches, Tom Jenkins.

65. Narberth Church School football team, 1925/26.
Back row (from left): Vivian Jenkins, ? Evans, Wilfred ? , Ralph Gaches, Reggie Griffiths, Tom Mathias.
Front row (from left): David Williams, Willie James, Harold John, ? , Bernard Smith.

66. Narberth Intermediate School, 1926. Younger pupils.

67. Narberth Intermediate school, 1926.

Back row : no names available

Third row (from left): Terry Davies, ? , ? , ? , ? , ? , ? , ? , ? , Mollie Garrett, ? , ? , Muriel Lewis.

Second row (from left): ? , ? , Gertie Morgan (Cookery), Miss Jones (P.T.), Katie Morgan (French), Charlie Jones (Geography), Tom Francis (Headmaster), ? , Miss Howells, Elsie Richards, Beryl Tribe, ?, Eirion Nicholas, Sarah Llewellyn,

Front row (from left): ? , Margaret Long, Maud Griffiths, Megan Williams, ? , Eluned Howells, Violet Rogers, Ruth Reynolds, Florence Rogers, ? , ? , ? .

68. Narberth Intermediate School production, c. 1930. Ron Cole (third from right, back row) is the only one who has been identified from this play.

69. Intermediate School outing, c.1920. Abel Jones recalls in his biography of the school's first headmaster that '. . . it was on the annual County School excursions to Saundersfoot that John Morgan would be at his happiest. He would invite the children and their parents, and pay the cost of the train and the food himself. Then friends began to invite their friends and their friends' friends, until the crowd ran into hundreds.'

PEOPLE

PEOPLE are the essence of Narberth. The sense of community is strong and much valued by those who live here, whether they have been here all their lives or have just moved to the area. The evidence of these photographs would seem to suggest that it has always been so.

One of the major differences in the lives of the people appearing in these early photographs is the nature of their work. At the turn of the century most residents would have found employment within the town. Apart from agriculture and trade, the local woollen mills were still providing work for a substantial number of people. J. Geraint Jenkins in his book *Life and Tradition in Rural Wales* describes how in Narberth at the end of the 19th century '. . . there were twelve woollen factories; the largest Landmill accommodated as many as forty power looms within it'. The industry flourished until the end of the First World War when the price of wool fell disastrously. One of the local mills at Gelli struggled on until 1938 where a fire destroyed the main buildings and production came to an end.

Within the town itself one of the major employers was the firm of James Williams and photographs of some of those who worked there appear in this section.

The firm began trading in the town around 1830. It was originally housed in what is now the museum in Market Square, and the brewing and bottling was carried out in the cellar. Barley was malted at the rear of the premises. The advent of the railway meant that beer and spirits could be brought in by rail, and the company flourished. Bottling was now carried out in the cellars as before and also in a warehouse on the opposite side of the Square. Related crafts including the making of baskets to cover the stone jars, and men were also employed to drive the drays and maintain the horses.

In 1896 the bonded stores was built in Church Street where whisky, port, rum and sherry were blended. The casks used were made from local timber from the Mill Pond, Shipping Factory and Lower Valley areas.

Throughout the early decades of the century the company acquired more and more licensed premises in Pembrokeshire and depots were opened in Pembroke, Pembroke Dock, Harverfordwest, Cardigan and Carmarthen. Changes in the management of the company ensured and by 1950 the bottling of Guinness moved to the Victoria Hall following a fire in the 'Guinness' Room in Water Street. In the following year all bottling was carried out there. It was in the early 1980s that the Hall was eventually demolished.

The James Williams firm continues as a major employer in Narberth, from its new premises in Spring Gardens. The museum, housed in the old offices of James Williams in Market Square, holds memorabilia and records covering its history.

Other photographs in this section depict some aspects of Narberth 'at play'.

Team sport has always been an important social activity. Rugby has been played here since about 1879 and an excellent description of the subsequent development of the game has been given in Dennis Irving's book *One Hundred Years of Rugby in Narberth*.

Soccer appears to have been here from the beginning of the century. The Parish Magazine for November 1901 reports that '. . . active steps are being taken towards the formation of a Football Club in Narberth . . . We hope to be able to report in our next issue that a good team has been formed and fixtures made'. Unfortunately no such report appears.

Narberth Cricket Club was in existence from 1870. In 1901 we find the Rev. John Morris lamenting, 'This popular English game is now being played all over the country. So far we have heard no talk of the Narberth Cricket Club. We hope it has not retired into the shades of obscurity. Narberth was able to boast of a fairly good team last season, and without doubt a splendid one could be formed this season. It appears there is some difficulty in getting a field . . .'

A tennis club was started in that year by Mrs J. D. Lewis, Greenway, to be held in the Victoria Hall during the Winter and Spring.

Today a much wider range of sporting facilities is available in the town—from the swimming pool to those on offer at Bloomfield Community Centre.

For those whose leisure interests lie elsewhere there have always been cultural activities. Many, especially in the early years of the century, were associated with the chapels and churches. Eisteddfodau and choral singing, debating societies, lectures and magic lantern shows are all frequently reported.

More secular entertainments also appear. The building of the Victoria Hall in 1897 was a tremendous boost to the provision of concerts. Writing in November that year, the Rector noted, 'Since the opening of our spacious Victoria Hall our little town has been well supplied with entertainments, most of them of a high class. This remark specially applies to the last given there by Herr Pareezer's Prussian Choir. This Company occupied the Hall for a week, attracting good audiences throughout. The tone of the entire series of entertainments, different nightly, was excellent, and the performances of the various artistes most praiseworthy. The various entertainments were illustrated by some beautiful Dioramic Views.'

Since then Narberth's reputation as a centre for good entertainment has continued.

Reference has been made in the captions to the work of Sybil Noott in the 1930s and 40s. Amateur dramatic productions by the Penfro Players were also well received.

After the opening of the Queen's Hall in 1958 a whole new era of public performances ensued. In the late 1960s the hall featured many of the famous bands of the time. Henry Langen's excellent article in the December/January 1998/9 issue of *Pembrokeshire Life* describes how bands like Status Quo, Freddie and The Dreamers, Amen Corner and The Herd were booked, often before they had achieved national stardom. This was the golden age of entertainment for some sections of Narberth society.

Today the Queen's Hall regularly promotes a wide range of cultural activities suitable for all ages and tastes.

70. Great-granny Thomas, midwife, of Plaindealings Road and Lily Thomas, her grand-daughter.

71. Tennis party, around the turn of the century. Miss M. Howell (left, seated) and Miss B. Howell (right, seated) were members of the James Williams family.

72. Narberth junior rugby team, late 1920s.

Back row (from left): Rev. Rochford Williams, Llewellyn Griffiths, Ivor John, Dennis Irving, T.J.Waters, Wynford Christopher, Terry Davies, Arty Irving, Bryn Calvin Thomas, Mr Calvin Thomas, Rev. ? , Tommy Thomas.

Middle row (from left): Little boy (unnamed), Jim Williams, Brynmor Harries, Arthur Phillips, Arthur Tucker, Harold John.

Front row (from left): Charles Edwards, Clyde Richards, Roy John, Haydn Rowe.

73. Narberth soccer team, 1949.
 Back row (from left): Ernie Hoyland, Bobby De Winton, Colwyn Callan, Norman Morgan, Tommy James, Vincent Hallwood, ? Morgenstein, Stanley Jones, Jack Hallwood, Willie Evans.
 Front row (from left): Ivor Badham, 'Rolo' Reynolds, Keith Owen, Alun Young, Gwyn Perkins, Dennis Rossiter, Dennis Hallwood, ? , Mr A. E. Steadman.

74. Sybil Noott and one of her many dance troupes, c.1930s. Born in Aspatria, Cumbria, the second daughter of theatrical parents, Sybil Noott met and married Fred Noott, a Narberth jeweller, in 1930. She started a dance school in the town and produced *Red Riding Hood*, the first of many pantomimes, in 1936. These were staged in the Victoria Hall and in the Palace, Haverfordwest. After the war she was the driving force behind the local dramatic productions and received favourable reviews. One of her protegees, Eva Beynon, went on to sing with Ambrose and his dance orchestra.

From left: Ann Hedley, Margaret Jones, Aloe Rowlands, Glenda Reynolds, Shirley Jenkins, Joan Hedley, Mrs Noott, Morfydd Thomas, Elsie Thomas, Joyce Rowlands, Valerie Evans, Margaret Hughes, Thelma Lewis.

75. Sybil Noott's 'Merry Mites'.
   Back row (from left): Mair Morris, Stella Mathias, Betty Baker, Mary Watkins, Doreen Christopher, Megan Hughes, Nesta Davies, Margaret Rogers.
   Front row (from left): Barbara Watts, Anne Noott, Joyce Badham.

76. Sybil Noott's 'Dainty Blossoms', 1948.
   (From left) Aloe Rowlands, Janet Nicholas, Margaret Hughes, Thelma Lewis, Ann Hedley, Margaret Jones, Maureen Evans, Valerie Evans.

77. Sybil Noott's 'Violet Rays'.
   (From left): Rosemary Webb, Hilda Rees, Mary Nicholas, Gwen Duckfield, Dilys Irving, Margaret Mutlow, Gwen ? (an evacuee).

78. Sybil Noott's 'Rainbow Belles', 1948.
   (From left): Joan Williams, Joan Hedley, Joyce Rowlands, Glenda Reynolds, Merle Scourfield, Elsie Thomas, Morfydd Thomas, Shirley Jenkins.

79. Conservative Ladies Association, around the turn of the century.

80. Thought to be a gathering of the Mothers' Union, 1920s.

81. Red Cross nurses, taken in Miss Anderson's (centre front) garden, Templeton.

82. Group thought to be the Women's Legion, outside the Denant Cafe, High Street.
Front row (from left): ? , Mrs Jones, Miss Lewis Lloyd, Miss Lewis (Greenway), Miss Gertie Glyn, Miss Hilda Davies, ? , Miss Alie Owen.
Others recognised: Mrs Jack Thomas, Mrs Anthony, Mrs Gwyther, Mrs George Thomas, Miss Rogers, Mrs Farrow, Mrs Owen, Mrs Nicholas, Florrie Davies, Miss Lilian Bowen, Miss James (Blacksmith), Mrs Mathias, Mrs Billy Lewis, Phyllis Hughes, Mrs Bernard Smith, Nan Jones, Maudie Williams.

83. Baptist Chapel outing, August 1936.
(From left) Peggy Adams, Doreen Thomas, Peggy Jones, Islwyn Evans, Evelyn Davies, Olwen Webb, Bus Driver, Megan George.

84. GWR dray and horse delivering casks outside Rock House, late 1930s.
A. Gwyther (left) worked for the GWR, Tommy Jones (right) was employed by James Williams.

85. James Williams employees, possibly in the keg yard, c.1930.
Back row (from left): Trevor Jones, Islwyn Lewis ('Snowball'), ? , Howard Christopher (boy at back), Billy Gwyther, Gordon John.
Front row (from left): Tommy Jones ('Curley'), Ollie Evans, Harry Tucker, ? .

86. Group of James Williams employees, 1938.
Back row: ?, ? .
Middle row (from left): Edwin Evans, Billy Gwyther, Islwyn Lewis, Ollie Evans.
Front row (from left): Hugh Nicholas, Edford James.

87. Group of James Williams employees outside what is now the Museum, 1939.
   Back row (from left): Ollie Evans, Islwyn Lewis, Willie Gwyther, Bill Griffiths, Douglas Bevan, Hugh Nicholas, ? , Danny Nicholas, ? .
   Front row (from left): Edwin Evans, Norman Watts, Leslie Baker, ? .

88. 'Daffo' Lewis (right), Saddle, Collar and Harness Maker selling his wares at Narberth's hiring fair, 1930s. The auctioneer (standing right on cart) is Mr Jackie Williams of Market Street.

89. Lawrence and Phyllis Davies of Kiln Park Farm with their milk cart. The picture is taken outside the County Sessions Room in St James Street. Formerly the Wesleyan Chapel, it is now the library.

90. Mr Alfred George Owen outside his tailor's shop, 41 High Street, c. 1920s. The business had moved from Plaindealings Road at some time between 1914 and 1923. When the tailoring trade was hit by the increasing availability of ready-made clothes, the shop became a gown and mantle shop. It closed in 1979, and the building was demolished in 1989 to make way for the development of Queen's Court.

91. Women collecting water from the communal tap in Church Street, c. early 1930s: (From left) Miss Eileen Eynon, 'Auntie Maudie' (Mrs M. Williams), Mrs Llewellyn Thomas.

92. Ben John, 'Ben the Bus', and postman, Mr Robinson, in the Station Yard, c. mid-1930s. A famous figure in Narberth, Ben John operated the horse-drawn taxi service to and from the station for nearly forty years. When his last horse, Nancy, died in 1942 and he was forced to retire, poems appeared in the local press commemorating his service to the town.

93. Staff of Gelli Woollen Mill, 1909.

Front row (from left): William Thomas, Pollie Davies, Ellen James, Lizzie Thomas, Joe Phillips, Anne Thomas, Martha Davies holding Bob, the dog.

Second row (from left): John Isaac, Sarah Williams, Martha Harries, Rebecca Thomas, William Morris, Dai Thomas.

Third row (from left): Frank Lewis, David Jones, William Davies, William Watkin, Tommy Reynolds, Henry Williams, Tom Williams.

Fouth row (from left): Emrys Williams, Jack Williams, Johnny Jones, John Williams, Tommy Devonald, Tommy Williams, Jim Thomas.

CATALOGUE

STREETS

1. NARB 28-1999
Copy of photograph of W. John, From the collection of Mr Chris Edwards.

2. NARB 683
Copy of photograph from John Thomas collection, National Library of Wales, Aberystwyth.

3. NARB 680
Copy of photograph from John Thomas collection, National Library of Wales, Aberystwyth.

4. NARB 1356(c)
Postcard.' High Street - Narberth'. A. F. Halkon.

5. NARB 1491
Postcard. 'High Street, Narberth'. A. F. Halkon Stationer, Narberth. Red 1d George V stamp. Postmark Narberth 1922. Addressed to 'Mrs E. Gundersen, No 12, Villiers St, Velindra, Aberavon, Port Talbot.'

6. NARB 158
Postcard 'High Street. Narberth'. F. Frith & Co. Ltd., Reigate (NBTH 21)

7. NARB 92-1991
Postcard. No information.

8. NARB 82-1995
Postcard. No information.

9. NARB 64-1993
Postcard. 'High St. Narberth W.J.' Addressed to 'Mr E. L. Davies, Draper, Golden Sheaf, Narberth'.

10. NARB 94-1991
Postcard. 'Fair Day, Narberth'. Green ½d Edward VII stamp. Postmark Narberth 1904. Addressed to 'Miss E. Beynon, Gt Neeston, Milford Haven'.

11. NARB Ena Jones loan 2
Postcard. 'High Street, Narberth'. Mortimer Allen, Photo:, Tenby.

12. NARB 140-1993
Postcard. 'High Street. Narberth (NBTH 12a).

13. NARB 153
Postcard. 'Narberth'. A.F. Halkon, Narberth. Green ½d George V stamp. Postmark Begelly 1910. Addressed to Miss P. Pledge, Grosvenor House, Railway Street, Saundersfoot.

14. NARB 349
Postcard. No information.

15. NARB 96-1990
Postcard. 'Narberth'. A.F.Halkon. Green ½d George V stamp. Postmark Narberth 1912. Addressed to 'Miss Alice Thomas, 29, Brook St., Blaenrhondda, Treherbert'.

16. NARB 34-1990
Postcard.'Narberth, The Town Seats'. Frith (NBTH 25).

17. NARB 46-1991
Postcard. 'Plain Dealings Road, Narberth'. A. F. Halkon, Narberth.

18. NARB 137-1992
Postcard. 'Spring Gardens, Narberth'. Lilywhite (1932) Ltd., Sowerby Bridge.(Nbh 14). Red Silver Jubilee 1d George V stamp. Postmark Narberth 1935. Addressed to Miss H. Thomas, c/o Jones and Higgins, Rye Lane, London, S.E. 15.

19. NARB 399
Postcard. 'Spring Gardens. Narberth'. F. Frith & Co. Ltd., Reigate.

20. NARB 565
Postcard. No information.

21. NARB 97-1990
Postcard. 'Spring Gardens, Narberth'. A. F. Halkon.

22. NARB 39-1989
Postcard. 'Jesse's Road, Narberth'. Lilywhite (1932) Ltd., Sowerby Bridge (Nbh 17).

23. NARB 90-1992
    Postcard. 'Station Road, Narberth'. A. F. Halkon, Stationer, Narberth.
24. NARB 38-1989
    Postcard. 'Station Road, Narberth'. Lilywhite (1932) Ltd., Sowerby Bridge.
25. NARB 35-1990
    Postcard. 'Commercial Corner, Narberth'. F. Frith & Co. Ltd., Reigate.
26. NARB 1356(a)
    Postcard. 'Sheep Street, Narberth'. A. F. Halkon, Narberth. Addressed to 'Miss Lloyd, The Post Office, Clarbeston Road'.
27. NARB 10-1998
    Postcard. No information.
28. NARB 15-1999 (49)
    Postcard. 'St James St, Narberth'. Photo by H. Mortimer Allen, Tenby. Green ½d George V stamp. Postmark Narberth 1914. Addressed to 'Mr W. B. Stephens, Parc-y-Lan Inn, Llanddewi Velfrey, Narberth'.
29. NARB 128-1992
    Postcard. 'Narberth's Last Street Fair, 1910'. Mortimer Allen Photo., Tenby.
30. NARB 68-1991
    Postcard. 'St James St. Narberth'. Green ½d Edward VII stamp. Postmark illegible. Addressed to 'Mrs Tom John, Rock House, Penrhiwtyn, Neath, Glam'.
31. NARB 46-1994
    Postcard. 'Market Square, Narberth'. Mortimer Allen, Tenby.
32. NARB 178-1990
    Postcard. Stamp removed. Addressed to 'Miss M. John, Water Gate, Clynderwen'.
33. NARB 1362
    Postcard. 'Market Square, Narberth'. The Excelsior Photo Co., Ltd., Carmarthen. Stamp removed. Postmark Narberth 1907. Addressed to 'Mr. JOP.W. Davies, 28 Endymion Rd, Finsbury Pk., London'.
34. NARB 1363
    Postcard 'Market Square, Narberth'. A. F. Halkon.
35. NARB 1356
    Postcard. 'Court House, Narberth'. A. F. Halkon
36. NARB 215
    Postcard. No information.
37. NARB 179-1990
    Postcard. S.G.Griffiths, Haverfordwest and Milford Haven.
38. NARB 145-1990
    Postcard. 'St Andrew's Church, Narberth'. Published by A.F.Halkon, Stationer, Narberth. Brown ¾d George V stamp. Postmark 1922. Addressed to 'Mrs E. Gundersen, No 12, Villier Street, Velindra, Aberavon, Port Talbot'.
39. NARB 141-1993
    Postcard. 'The Baptist Church Narberth'. F. Frith & Co. Ltd., Reigate.(NBTH 17)
40. NARB 1496
    Postcard. 'Crinow Parish Church, Narberth'. Raphael Tuck & Sons'. (NBH 28)
41. NARB 555
    Postcard. 'Wesley Church, Narberth'. A. F Halkon, Narberth.
42. NARB 16-1999
    Copy of photograph from John Thomas collection, National Library of Wales, Aberystwyth.

CARNIVALS
43. NARB328
    Postcard. 'Narberth Carnival, 1906 W.J.'.
44. NARB 1192
    Postcard. 'Narberth Carnival, 1906 W.J.'.
45. NARB 62-1991
    Postcard. 'Narberth Carnival 1909. Photo by W. John, Clynderwen'.

46. NARB 149-1992
     Postcard. 'Carnival Group, Narberth 1907'.
47. NARB 1196
     Postcard. 'Narberth Carnival 1907 W. G. Morris'.
48. NARB 150-1992
     Postcard. No Information.
49. NARB 148-1992
     Postcard. No information.
50. NARB 152-1992
     Postcard. No information.
51. NARB 151-1992
     Postcard. Photo by W. John, Clynderwen, Pem.
52. NARB 64-1991
     Postcard. No information.
53. NARB 1206
     Postcard. 'Photo by W.John, Clynderwen'.
54. NARB 50-1991
     Postcard. H. Mortimer Allen, Tenby.
55. NARB 69-1991
     Postcard. H. Mortimer Allen, Tenby.
56. NARB Ena Jones loan 4
     Postcard. '1907'.
57. NARB 130-1997
     Postcard. 'Narberth Carnival 1919'.
58. NARB 337
     Postcard. Squibbs, Tenby and Pembroke Dock.

SCHOOLS
59. NARB 350
     Postcard. No information.
60. NARB 22-1995
     Postcard. No information
61. NARB 126-1992
     Postcard. No information.
62. NARB 346
     Postcard. No information.

63. NARB 345
     Postcard. No information.
64. NARB 49-1991
     Postcard. No information.
65. NARB 582
     Postcard. No information.
66. NARB 343
     Postcard. No information.
67. NARB 49-1992
     Postcard. No information.
68. NARB 342
     Postcard. No information.
69. NARB 340
     Postcard. No information.

PEOPLE
70. NARB 124-1992
     Postcard. Photo by W. John, Clynderwen, Pem.
71. NARB 1209
     Postcard. No information.
72. NARB 202-1990
     Postcard. No information.
73. NARB 1423(a)
     Postcard. 'Studio Janiven', (S. RobinShaw), 9 Mary St, Milford Haven.
74. NARB 318
     Postcard. No information.
75. NARB 12-1996
     Postcard. No information.
76. NARB 93-1992
     Postcard. No information
77. NARB 129-1997
     Postcard. Squibbs, Photographer, Tenby and Pembroke Dock.
78. NARB 94-1992
     Postcard. No information.

79. NARB 1497

Postcard. No information. Note that the postcard has been printed back to front.

80. NARB 525

Postcard. No information.

81. NARB 561

Postcard. No information.

82. NARB 190

Postcard. *Western Telegraph.*

83. NARB 67-1998

Postcard. Jerome Ltd.

84. NARB 35-1996

Postcard. Jerome Ltd.

85. NARB 1498

Postcard. No information.

86. NARB 15-1994

Postcard. No information.

87. NARB 1210

Postcard. No information.

88. NARB 127-1992

'Narberth 11'. H. Mortimer Allen, Tenby.

89. NARB 380

Postcard. No information.

90. NARB 52-1998

Copy of photograph from the collection of Miss E. Owen.

91. NARB 386

Copy of photograph from the collection of Mrs E. Phillips.

92. NARB 1264

Photograph from the Ben John family collection.

93. NARB 28-1995

Photograph taken by W. John of Clynderwen.

94. [Front Cover] Photograph of W. John's camera, a 'Special' patent camera, made by J. Lancaster of Birmingham.